My Ne

David Bauer

Illustrated by Kathleen Rietz

Rigby®

A Harcourt Achieve Imprint

www.Rigby.com
1-800-531-5015

Look at the ball.

Look at the rope.

Look at the bowl.

Look at the collar.

Look at the bed.

Look at the bone.

Look at the wagon!

Look at the dog!